WORLD ADVENTURES

BY STEFFI CAVELL-CLARKE

©2018
Book Life
King's Lynn
Norfolk PE30 4LS

ISBN: 978-1-78637-242-0

All rights reserved
Printed in Malaysia

Written by:
Steffi Cavell-Clarke

Edited by:
Kirsty Holmes

Designed by:
Dan Scase

A catalogue record for this book is available from the British Library.

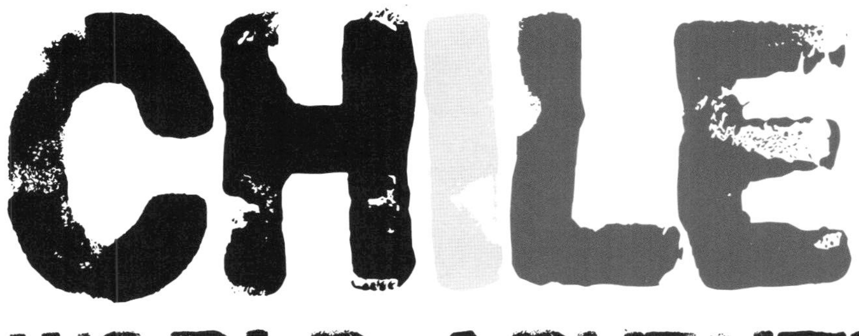

WORLD ADVENTURES

CONTENTS

Words in **red** can be found in the glossary on page 24.

WHERE IS CHILE?

Chile is a long, narrow country that stretches along the western side of South America.

COLOMBIA

BRAZIL

CHILE

SANTIAGO

ARGENTINA

The population of Chile is around 18 million. Most people live in towns and cities. Around seven million people live in the capital city of Chile.

The capital city of Chile is called Santiago.

WEATHER AND LANDSCAPE

The weather in Chile changes across the country. It is usually hot and dry in the north, and cool and wet in the south.

There are many different landscapes in Chile. It has hot deserts, cool rainforests and long **mountain ranges**.

Chile has around 500 **active volcanoes**.

CLOTHING

Most Chilean people wear casual clothing, such as jeans and T-shirts. Many people also wear a **traditional** piece of clothing called a poncho.

Some people dress up in traditional clothes for **festivals** and parties. Women wear a Chilean huaso dress and men wear a straw hat called a chupalla.

RELIGION

There are many different **religions** that people follow. The religion with the most followers in Chile is Christianity. Most Christians in Chile are **Roman Catholic**.

The Roman Catholic place of **worship** is a church. Most Catholics visit a church every Sunday.

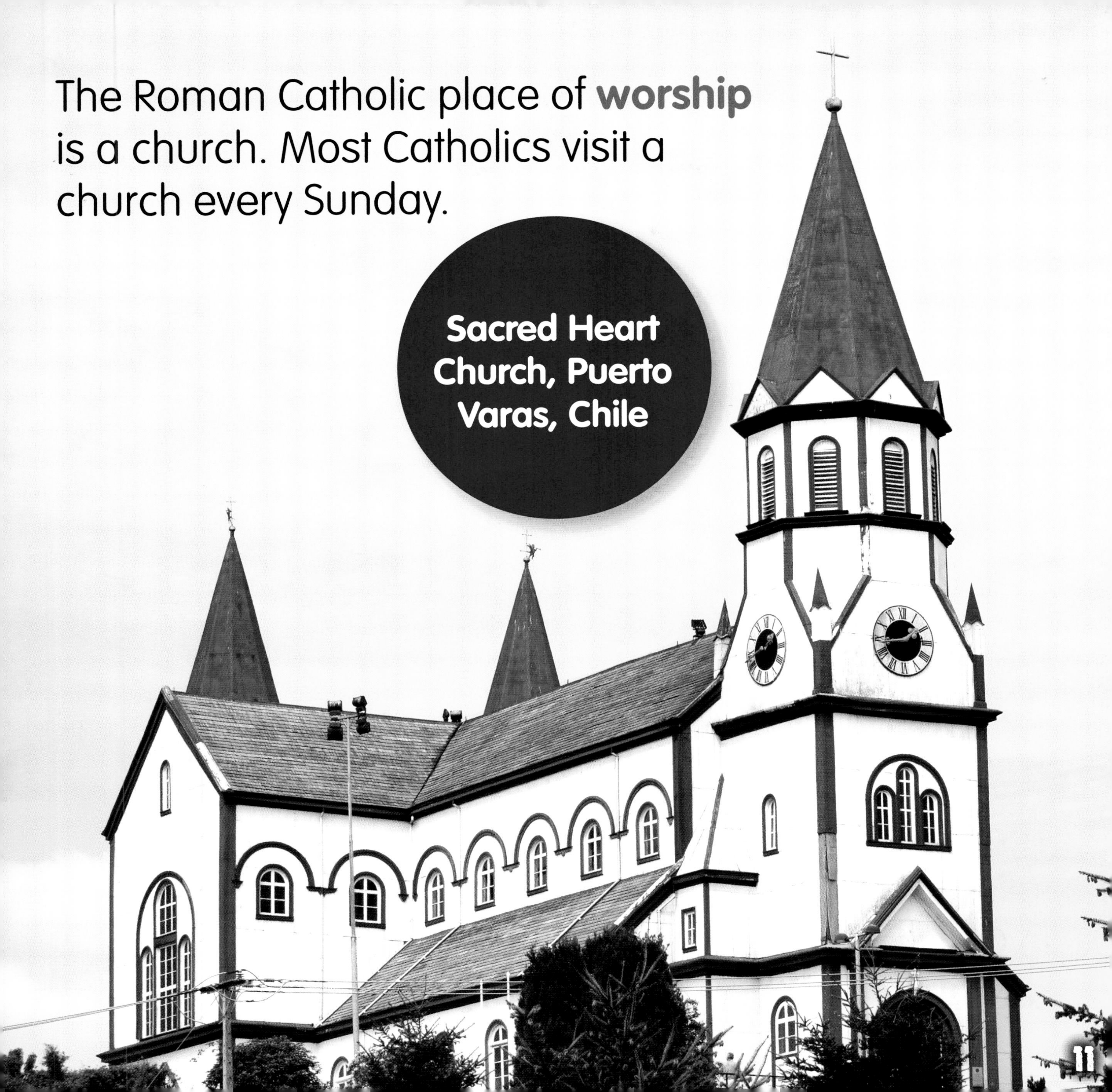

Sacred Heart Church, Puerto Varas, Chile

FOOD

Chile has a wide range of different types of food to eat. It has seafood, meat, bread, fresh fruit and vegetables.

The pastel de choclo is a traditional dish in Chile. It is a type of pie made with corn, vegetables, chicken and beef.

AT SCHOOL

In Chile, children start school at 6 years old and study until they are 18 years old. At school, most children have to wear a school uniform.

Children in Chile study Spanish, English, maths, science and history. Most children go to school to study, but some children are taught at home.

AT HOME

SANTIAGO, CHILE

Many people in Chile live in or near to big cities where there are lots of jobs. In cities like Santiago, most of the people live in **modern** flats.

Lots of people in Chile also live in the countryside. Many famers grow lots of fruit there, such as grapes, apples and peaches.

FAMILIES

Most children live with their parents, brothers and sisters, or other family members like grandparents.

In Chile, families often get together to celebrate religious events, such as Christmas and Easter.

SPORT

Fans supporting their favourite football team.

Sports, such as basketball, tennis, football and rugby are very popular in Chile.

Rodeo is a traditional sport in Chile. In a Chilean rodeo, two riders on horses try to capture a young cow, called a calf, with long ropes.

FUN FACTS

The **national** dance of Chile is called the cueca.

In the cueca, a woman and a man wear traditional Chilean clothes and dance together without touching one another.

There is an island off the coast of Chile called Easter Island. It is famous for having 887 massive statues, called mo'ai.

The mo'ai statues on Easter Island.

GLOSSARY

active volcanoes	a mountain that could erupt with lava and gas
festivals	times when people come together to celebrate special events
modern	something from present or recent times
mountain ranges	a group of connected mountains
national	relating to, characteristic of or common to a nation
population	number of people living in a place
religions	systems of faith and worship
Roman Catholic	a member of the Roman Catholic church
traditional	things people have done in a certain way for a long time
worship	a religious act, such as praying

Photocredits: Abbreviations: l-left, r-right, b-bottom, t-top, c-centre, m-middle.
Front Cover – Dmytro Vietrov, bg – Aleksey Klints. 1 – Aleksey Klints. 2 – kavram. 3 – Dmytro Vietrov. 5 – Jose Luis Stephens. 6 – Helder Geraldo Ribeiro. 7 – Grey82. 8 – Kalmatsuy. 9 – MARCELODLT. 10 – DenisFilm. 11 – marktucan. 12tr – Larisa Blinova, 12tl – Pablo Rogat, 12bl – By Pablo Rogat, 12mb – Avdeyukphoto, 12br – Ildi Papp. 13 – Ildi Papp. 14 – India Picture. 15 – wavebreakmedia. 16 – Pablo Rogat. 17 – Shch. 18 – Monkey Business Images. 19 – Monkey Business Images. 20 – AGIF. 21 – Tomas Skopal. 22 – Fotocrisis. 23 – Gabor Kovacs Photography. Images are courtesy of Shutterstock.com. With thanks to Getty Images, Thinkstock Photo and iStockphoto.